Looking Back at
Clothes and Fashion

SCHOOLHOUSE
PRESS

Copyright © 1988 by Schoolhouse Press, Inc.
160 Gould Street, Needham
Massachusetts 02194
ISBN 0-8086-1177-1 (hardback)
ISBN 0-8086-1184-4 (paperback)

Original copyright, © Macmillan Education Limited 1988

Author: Anne Mountfield

Editorial planning by AMR

Designed and typeset by The Pen and Ink Book Company
Ltd, London

Illustrations by Jane Cheswright, Frank James, Douglas Hall,
Sally Launder, Kay Dixey

Picture research by Liz Rudoff

Printed in Hong Kong

Library of Congress Cataloging-in-Publication Data

Looking back at clothes and fashion.

  Includes index.
    1. Clothing and dress--History--Juvenile literature.
2. Fashion--History--Juvenile literature.   I. Schoolhouse
Press.   II. Title: Clothes and fashion.
GT511.L66 1988   391   87-15346
ISBN 0-8086-1177-1
ISBN 0-8086-1184-4 (pbk.)

Note to the reader
In this book there are some words in the text which are printed in **bold** type. This shows that the
word is listed in the glossary on page 46. The glossary gives a brief explanation of words which
may be new to you.

Photographic Credits

t=top b=bottom l=left r=right

The author and publishers wish to acknowledge,
with thanks, the following photographic sources:
title, (Victoria and Albert Museum, London); 18,
19*t*, 21*t*, 29*t*, 43, Bridgeman Art Library, London;
contents, 13*b*, 21*b*, 25*t* and *b*, 29*b*, 39*t* and *b*, Mary
Evans Picture Library, London; 5*l*, 26*l*, (British
Museum); 34 (L.J. Anderson Collection); Werner
Forman Archive, London; 5*r*, 22, 32, Michael
Holford; 8, 10, 31*b*, Hutchison Photograph
Library, London; 16, 17, I.C.I. Fibres Division; 4,
9*b*, 11*r*, 23*b*, Peter Newark's Western Americana;
19*b*, (photograph Matteini), Rex Features,
London; 16-17, 40, Ann Ronan; 38, Scala, Italy;
35, (photograph David Leah), Science Photo
Library, London; 31*t*, Victoria and Albert
Museum, London; 6, 7*l* and *r*, 9*t*, 11*l*, 14, 15, 26*r*,
34-35, 36, 37, 41*l* and *r*, 42, Zefa, UK;
Cover photograph courtesy of Bridgeman Art
Library and The Victoria and Albert Museum,
London
The publishers have made every effort to trace
the copyright holders, but if they have
inadvertently overlooked any, they will be
pleased to make the necessary arrangements at
the first opportunity.

Contents

Introduction

People wear clothing for many reasons. Some people live in cold places. They need to keep warm. Other people live in hot countries and need to cover their skin, so that the sun does not burn it. In places where the weather often changes, people need to change the kind of clothing they wear. Also, what people wear depends on what they are doing.

▲ This picture of Native Americans was painted over one hundred years ago. Most of their clothing is made of animal hides. The cloaks are worn with the fur inside. The outside is decorated. The Iroquois in the center is wearing a woven blanket and woven belt.

The First Clothing

When hunters wore animal hides, they found that the hides kept them warm. In cold countries, people began to wear fur clothing. They learned to sew the fur together. They used needles made from the bones of animals or fish. The thread was made from strips of leather or from the stems of plants.

In hot countries, the sun kept people warm. People did not need a lot of clothing. Sometimes, they wore a kind of apron, made from the bark of trees. Sometimes, they made skirts by tying leaves or grasses together. Clothing was worn mostly for decoration. Long, loose clothing also helped to protect people's bodies from the sun.

Perhaps, people first wore clothing as a form of magic, too. They painted their faces and made patterns on their skin. They thought that this would frighten away their enemies. They also thought that it would keep away evil spirits. People also wore lucky charms, called **amulets**. These were made from the bones, claws, and teeth of animals, or from wood or stone. People believed that spirits lived in animals, plants, and rocks. Hunters killed wild animals and wore their hides. They believed that wearing the hide would make them strong like the animals.

Belts and necklaces are some of the oldest forms of clothing. They were used to hang amulets around people's waists or necks. Belts could also be used for carrying hunting weapons and tools.

▲ The tribes of the plains of North America made necklaces like this. There are bear claws attached to it. Only the bravest men were allowed to wear bear claws.

Making Clothes

People learned to spin thread and to weave the thread into cloth. In some places, they used the wool from the animals they kept. In other places, they made cloth from plants, such as cotton or flax. The Chinese made cloth from a silk thread spun by silkworms.

Cloth was easy to cut and sew. It could be cut and made to fit the shape of the body. This is called **tailoring**. In hot countries, cloth was often **draped** in folds around the body. Draped clothing is cool to wear in warm weather because it does not fit close to the body.

▼ This statue shows how a young girl from a wealthy family dressed about 2,000 years ago in Roman times. The material of her dress is draped in folds around her body.

Keeping Warm and Cool

Hundreds of thousands of years ago, the northern half of the earth was covered by ice. People could not live there. They lived in the warm, green lands of the south, in places like Africa. When they learned to make fire and to wear animal hides, they could keep warm. They began to move north.

Clothing for Warmth

One way to keep warm, in the past, was to cover the body with mud. Animal hides were also warm, but they soon dried out and became stiff. At first, people tried to soften the hides by chewing them or hammering them. Then, they found that they could soften the hides by rubbing them with oils. People also softened the hides by soaking them. They used a liquid from the bark of trees. Softening hides is called **tanning**. Tanning made the hides soft enough to sew.

Cave paintings of hunters have been found which are thousands of years old. They show that the hunters wore hooded jackets. Those jackets are very much like the ones that some Inuit people wear today. Until about forty years ago, wearing animal furs was the only way to keep warm in the frozen lands of the north. Soldiers who went there to fight wore the same clothing as the Inuit. The army paid Inuit women to make fur

▲ The Inuit people live in the far north. They need very warm clothing. Some still wear fur jackets and boots as their ancestors did. They also wear modern clothing. These men are wearing pants made of ordinary cloth.

clothes for them. Now, furs can be made in factories. They look like animal furs, but they are not made from hides. These artificial furs are light to wear, and cost less to buy than real furs.

Clothing to Keep Cool

Long ago, people in hot countries kept cool by wearing very little clothing. Animal hides were too hot and too heavy to wear as protection from the sun. Important people were often fanned with feathers or leaves to keep them cool also.

When people learned to make cloth, they could cover themselves with light clothing. Clothing helped to keep the sun from burning their skins. In India, some women drape a long length of cloth, called a **sari**, around their bodies. In Malaysia, men and women wrap a strip of cloth around their bodies. The loose end is tucked in at the waist, or under the arms. This strip of cloth is called a **sarong**. Near dry, sandy deserts, people wear flowing robes in the daytime. These robes allow the air to blow through them. In this way, people are kept cool. Sometimes, desert people wear a mask of cloth over their mouths. This keeps out sand and dust. At night, it is cold in the desert. People wrap themselves in blankets to keep warm.

▼ These women are from Bali, in Indonesia. Their skirts are made from long strips of cloth called sarongs. They may be made of silk or cotton. They are about four yards long, and are usually in very beautiful colors.

◄ The Tuareg people live in the Sahara Desert. The men wear turbans. They wrap the cloth around their heads and faces. This protects them from sandstorms. The clothing they wear is loose, so they can stay cool in the desert heat.

Decency and Decoration

People have very different ideas about what to wear. There are people who live deep in the forests of hot countries. They wear only a belt or a lip ornament. That is their way of dressing.

Decency

People's religions also tell them how to dress. In parts of the Middle East, people cover up all of their bodies. They do not like people to see their bodies. The

▲ In some Middle Eastern countries, women keep their faces and their heads covered. This woman is a Bedouin. She is wearing a special veil over her face called a yashmak. A Bedouin woman will not let any man except her husband see her face.

women cover their faces with veils, too. Sikh men, in India, wear a long piece of cloth on their heads. They wind it into a **turban**. Jewish men cover their heads when they pray. Muslims leave their shoes outside a temple. They worship barefoot. Some Buddhist priests wear orange robes. Some Christian women cover their heads when they go to church. Many brides, all over the world, still cover their faces with a veil on their wedding day.

Decoration

Some groups of people like to paint their faces and make patterns on their bodies. For thousands of years, they have decorated their bodies in these ways. Sometimes, the patterns were cut into the skin. The cuts were often stained with dye. Sometimes, they were made by pricking the skin with a needle. Colored dye was put into the needle holes. These patterns are called **tattoos**. Even before they knew how to make clothing, people put flowers and feathers in their hair. They wore necklaces made from shells, seeds, or bones.

People have also decorated their clothing. They painted patterns on animal hides. Sometimes, they cut the ends of the hides into strips, or a fringe. Beads were sewn on to hide clothing. Cloth was woven in patterns or dyed. Often, it was stitched with colored threads. A pattern sewn with colored

▶ These dancers are from Papua New Guinea. They have decorated their bodies and their faces. They have used mud, paint, and charcoal or ash to make different patterns.

threads is called **embroidery**. The patterns on the cloth might have circles and triangles. These were often like the patterns on body tattoos.

Trimmings were added to clothing as well. Ribbons, lace, even gold and jewels, were stitched on the cloth. The collars and sleeves might be edged with fur. People began to sell each other fine cloth, or **fabric**, and trimmings.

Some people like to be noticed. They like wearing clothing in styles that are new, or "in fashion." Early ideas of fashion started with the decoration of the body and clothes.

▲ Native Americans made beautiful garments from a soft leather called buckskin. They decorated their garments with fringes, beads, and dyes. This shirt made by the Sioux people has weasel skins stitched to it. These show that the wearer was an important person.

Natural Materials

People first made clothing from plants or animal hides. These are **natural materials**. They come from things that live and grow. People used whatever they could find. Some materials, like leaves, could be worn just as they were. Some, like animal hides, had to be softened to make them comfortable to wear. Other materials, like wool, had to be spun into thread. The thread was woven into cloth.

Trees, Leaves, and Grasses

In hot, damp forests, many plants have large leaves. People tied leaves together and made skirts. Grasses were woven into belts or made into skirts. Some people still wear clothes made in this way. In Samoa, skirts are made from leaves. In Hawaii, they are made from grass.

In Africa and South America, the inside of the bark of trees was used to make clothes. It was beaten until it was thin. Then, it was soaked and cut into strips. The strips were laid on top of each other. As they dried out, they stuck together. When the bark dried out, it was soft. It made a kind of cloth. It was used to make simple clothing.

Plants

Many plants have parts which are long and stringy. These are called **fibers**. People learned to use plant fibers to make cloth. In ancient Egypt, flax stalks were made into cloth. Aztec women, in South America, used the leaves of a cactus plant.

▼ These men are from the Solomon Islands in the Pacific Ocean. They wear grass skirts for traditional dancing. Most of the time, they wear modern clothes. You can see that they have shorts on under their skirts.

▲ The cotton plant grows in hot countries. It is a small bush. Its seeds grow in a kind of pod called a boll. This boll is filled with white, fluffy, fibers. These are used to make cotton thread.

Cotton grows in the hot, damp areas of Asia, Africa and the United States. White, silky hairs grow around the seeds of the cotton plant. Cotton thread can be made from these silky hairs.

Animals

Long ago, people made clothing from the hides of the animals they hunted. The tribes of North America wore buffalo, deer, beaver, and fox hides. The Inuit people hunted caribou and seal. In Central Asia and Northern Europe, people wore the skins of sheep and goats. They used calfskins to make leather for shoes.

People learned to use the animals' hairs, too. They made them into woollen thread. Then, they made the threads into cloth. They used hair from sheep, goats, camels, and llamas. Animal hairs could also be pressed together. The pressed hair made a cloth called **felt**.

In China, 5,000 years ago, people knew how to make silk. Silk comes from the case, or **cocoon**, that a silkworm makes around itself before it turns into a moth. The silkworms were kept on special "silk farms." Silk cloth is very thin and light. It can be draped and folded. Many saris are made of silk. Silk can also be cut and made into shirts, dresses, or scarves.

▼ The Sioux hunted the buffalo. They used the hides for clothing and to make tents. The women scraped these hides, cleaned, tanned them, and dried them out. It took six days to tan one hide.

11

Tools and Machines

Needles are the oldest tools used for making clothing. The first needles were made from bones or animal horn. Bone needles have been found that are 40,000 years old. Metal needles were made about 5,000 years ago. We know that metal scissors were made about 2,000 years ago. Needles and scissors are still used today. Their shape has not changed at all.

Spinning

One of the first tools for making thread was called a **distaff**. The distaff is a long wooden stick with a groove cut in one end. It is held under one arm. A lump of raw wool or plant fiber is pushed on to the distaff. The loose ends of the fibers are joined together and twisted around a bar of wood with a pin in it. This smaller stick was called the **spindle**. The spindle had a weight on it. This twisted around and around. As it turned, it pulled out the fibers into a long thread. This is called spinning the thread. The thread, or **yarn**, was wound around the bottom of the spindle. Many people still spin in this way.

For more than 500 years, wooden spinning wheels have often been used to turn the spindles. The yarn was spun at home by women.

In 1764, a British cloth maker, named James Hargreaves, invented a spinning machine. It was called the "Spinning

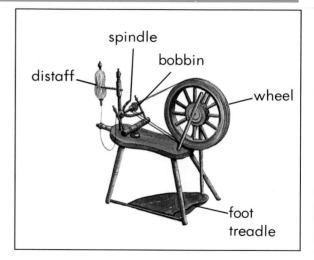

▲ The first spinning wheels probably came from India. The wheel was turned by hand. In the 1700's, there was a new kind of spinning wheel. This one had a treadle. The person spinning could work the treadle with their feet to make the wheel turn.

Jenny." "Jenny" was a short word for engine. With this machine, one person could spin several threads at once. Thread could be made very fast.

Weaving

The thread was woven into cloth. The cloth was made on a wooden frame called a **loom**. Two sets of thread were needed. One set of thread, called the **warp**, was held in place by the loom. The second set of thread was called the **weft**. It was wound around a small pointed holder called a **shuttle**. The weavers passed the shuttle over one warp thread and under the next. As the shuttle went across, and then back, it made rows of weft threads. The weavers pushed the rows of weft threads together by hand. This is how the cloth was made.

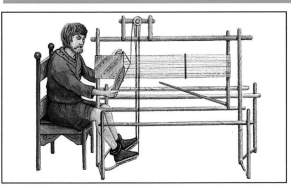

▲ This weaver is working on a loom. He is passing the shuttle carrying the weft thread between the warp threads.

About 200 years ago, looms were built that ran on water and steam power. Huge factories were built along the banks of rivers. In many countries, spinning and weaving no longer took place at home. Cloth making was quicker and easier in factories.

Sewing Machines

For thousands of years, clothing was sewn by hand. Then, about 200 years ago, sewing machines were invented. Isaac Merrit Singer, an American, first sold sewing machines in 1852. These machines had a wheel which the sewer turned. It made the needle go up and down. Sewing machines could sew hundreds of stitches in a minute. Today, factory machines sew thousands of stitches in a minute. The sewer does not turn the wheel by hand anymore. The machines work by electricity.

▼ This type of sewing machine was used in 1905. The design did not change for a long time. There are still plenty of machines like this today. They work by using a treadle. The person sewing has both hands free to hold the cloth.

Folk Costume

What are you wearing today? What would your clothing tell the people you meet? Would they know where you came from by how you dressed? People who lived in the same place used to wear the same kind of clothing. Sometimes, people knew which village strangers lived in by the style of their hats or the color of their skirts. Clothing which was worn in the past by particular groups of people is called folk costumes.

American Folk Costume

True American folk costume is the clothing of the Native Americans. Tribal costumes can be very different. In the northeast, the Mohawk tribe had one type of costume. The men wore a deerskin shirt, tight black leggings and **moccasins**. They shaved their heads, leaving only a long piece of hair on top. This was the scalp lock. The Mohawks attached a single feather to the scalp lock.

The women of the Zuni tribe in the southwest, wore dresses made of black cloth. They wore red or green belts. They also wore leggings and boots of white deerskin. The Zuni also wore beautiful turquoise jewelry, for which they are famous.

Today, there are many other types of folk costume in the United States. Many people who came to live in America brought their native costumes with them. In Texas or New Mexico, people might wear costumes that came from Spain. In Wisconsin and Minnesota, there are many people whose families came from one of the Scandanavian countries, like Sweden. They might wear their Scandanavian folk costumes during festivals or holidays. In large cities like New York, you may see people from

◀ People brought these costumes with them from many other places. Today they are mainly worn for special festivals. This costume is from the Ukraine.

▲ These Iranian women are wearing traditional clothes. They will only wear these clothes on special occasions, such as weddings. They usually wear a long black robe called a chador.

India, Saudi Arabia, or Japan, wearing their native clothing. Many people whose families came from Scotland still wear a pleated skirt called a **kilt**, to clan meetings all over the country. One group of people called the Amish still wear the simple, dark clothing that their ancestors wore. Most of the Amish came from Germany and settled in Pennsylvania. In Alaska, the Aleuts wear fur parkas, and the Hawaiians wear grass skirts.

Costumes in Asia and Africa

In many parts of the world, clothing has not changed very much at all. In India, women still wear saris made of cotton or silk, or trousers and long

tunics. In the Middle East, many men still wear long robes with a cloth covering the head. In China and Japan, some people still wear dark jackets and pants to work in. On special days, they might wear a long silk robe. In Japan, this is called a **kimono**. These robes are often embroidered. Today, western styles, like jeans and T-shirts, are worn in towns all over the world. These factory-made clothes are cheap, but they mean that colorful folk costumes are not worn as much as they were.

▼ Women in India have been wearing saris for over 2,000 years. Often, they are made of cotton printed with patterns which are only found in one area.

New Materials

Until about 200 years ago, most people wore cloth which was made at home or near where they lived. It was called **homespun** cloth. Local materials, such as sheep's wool, were used to make it. Chinese silks and Indian cottons cost a lot of money. They had to be carried long distances over the land and the sea.

Then, machines made it quick and easy to make cloth. Trains and steamships brought fabrics from around the world. The fabrics were less expensive now. This made more and more people able to buy them. So more cloth was needed. How could it be made more quickly and at a lower price?

New Cloth from Plants

In 1663, an English scientist, Robert Hooke, had the idea of spinning gum into thread. About 200 years later, this idea was tried. Scientists used wood pulp, or **cellulose**. It is a natural material and is found in plants. The scientists turned the cellulose into a liquid and heated it. Then, they poured it through very fine holes. The liquid became hard and turned into threads.

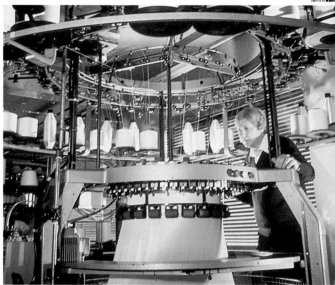

▲ Today, there are many kinds of synthetic fibers. They are made from chemical mixtures. Most synthetic fabrics are less expensive than natural fabrics. This factory in Britain is making a fabric which is used for sportswear.

Rayon

Fibers which are made by people are called **synthetics**. In 1889, a Frenchman, named Hilaire de Chardonnet, made a new material. It looked like silk. Chardonnet used wood pulp and **nitric acid**, but it kept exploding! Then, a safer way to make the material was found. People called the new thread "rayon." It was strong and did not cost a lot of money. Today, many fabrics have rayon in them. This is mixed with other fibers such as cotton or wool.

Nylon

Nylon was invented in the United States in the 1930's. Scientists mixed **chemicals** from coal tar and oil. Nylon was the first fiber to be made in this way. There are now many other fibers of this type. They are strong, wash easily, and keep their shape.

Synthetic materials are not expensive to make. Today, garments like shirts, sweaters, and raincoats can be made out of these new materials. In the future, the world's oil may become scarce. Then, people will have to invent new ways to make material for clothing.

▼ Skiers have to have clothing that is warm, light, and strong. It also needs to be flexible. Today, synthetic fabrics can do all these things. They can be made in bright colors as well.

◀ These men are working in a factory in France in 1898. They are making Chardonnet silk. This was the first kind of rayon. Working in the factory could be dangerous. The chemicals they were using caught fire easily and exploded.

Changing Fashions

What is fashion? It is a style of dressing which many people like to wear. Most fashions used to begin at the courts of kings and queens. Important people rushed to copy the latest styles. This court clothing was very expensive. It was often worn to impress other people. Often, this clothing was decorated with jewels and gold thread.

About 200 years ago, Marie Antoinette was Queen of France. Rose Bertin designed the queen's clothing. Each month, she sent fashion dolls to other courts. The dolls were dressed in the queen's latest styles. People copied these styles. Soon, the French court determined fashion in Europe and America.

Styles from Other Countries

In some countries, the styles in clothing have changed very slowly. Wealthier people in the Middle East, China, and India wore more elaborately decorated clothing than most people. But the styles were very much the same for rich and poor alike. The styles suited the way people lived in those places. Their way of life stayed the same for hundreds of years.

In Europe, the styles and shapes of clothing changed faster after the 1200's. New ideas often came from travelers. They had seen different clothing in other parts of the world. During the 1100's and 1200's, knights from Europe traveled to wars in the Middle East. These wars are known as the **Crusades**. The knights brought back some new styles to Europe. Women in Europe began to wear veils like the women in the Middle East did.

People who make up new styles are called designers. Often, they copy the styles and fabrics used in other countries. Chinese silk and shawls that were made in Kashmir in India have been used for a long time. They are still very popular today.

◀ Marie Antoinette was Queen of France in the late 1700's. She was famous for the amount of money she spent on clothing. The dress she is wearing in this painting was designed just for her. The outfits were made of silk. They were decorated with jewels.

▲ These Japanese women are wearing kimonos. The kimono is a traditional Japanese dress. It is similar to a light bathrobe. It is worn with a piece of cloth wrapped around as a very wide sash. Only young women had kimonos with these very long sleeves.

Laws about Fashion

Before 1600, there were laws in Europe about fashion. These laws were made to keep power and prestige. Rich merchants and their families could not wear silks and furs.

Another law about clothing was made in Britain. It was passed to help the sale of wool. All men had to own a woollen cape. They had to wear them on Sundays.

The Fashion Industry

When people make, buy, and sell one kind of thing, we say it is an **industry**. The fashion industry of today began in Paris. Rose Bertin is the first dress designer whose name we know. In 1858, another royal designer, Charles Worth, began selling clothing in Paris.

French designers such as Christian Dior and Coco Chanel were leaders of fashion about thirty years ago. Today, many countries have fashion industries. France, Italy, the US, Japan, and Britain lead the world in clothing design. New styles are put on show for summer and winter. Fashion shows are held in many countries. Shortly after these shows, cheaper ready-to-wear copies of the clothing can be found in local stores.

▲ Today, fashion is big business. Designers show their ideas to buyers at fashion shows.

The Shape of Clothing

The first clothing we know about was very simple in shape. Sometimes, the cloth was not cut at all. People folded or draped it around their bodies.

Draped Clothing

Cloth can be draped to make a cape, a skirt, or a scarf. Saris are a kind of dress made by draping. A strip of cloth, five to six yards long, is folded and draped around the body.

▲ Roman togas were often so long that they were awkward to wear.

About two thousand years ago, Roman men wore loose garments called **togas**. A toga was made from woollen cloth. It was folded around the body and the right arm was left free. Togas became very large. Some measured seven yards across.

Tailored Clothing

Clothing which has been cut into shapes is called tailored clothing. The first tailored clothing was simple. In Central and South America, people cut a hole in the middle of a piece of cloth. They put it on over their heads. It hung down over the shoulders. The garments are called **ponchos**. They are often made of wool and are very warm. All over the world, simple tunics were made by joining two pieces of cloth at the shoulders and at the sides. The tunics could be belted around the waist. Sleeves, hoods, and collars were later added if they were needed.

Changing Shape

In some places, the shape of clothing has changed very slowly. In China and Japan, women and men wore loose, long-sleeved gowns. These gowns had no collars. They were belted at the waist. The basic shape remained the same for thousands of years.

▶ This painting shows an archery contest in China in the 1700's. The government officials are all wearing the same kind of clothes. These are silk robes with square panels on the front and back. The style of the panel showed how important the wearer was.

In Europe, about 600 years ago, men and women often wore two tunics. The tunic worn under the outer tunic was longer. In time, women's longer tunics became skirts and dresses. The short tunics worn on top became blouses and jackets. About 500 years ago, men's top tunics were called **doublets**. This was because they were made from double layers of cloth with padding in between. Up to one hundred years ago, men and women still wore cloaks, not tailored coats, out of doors.

For hundreds of years, men wore short pants called **breeches**, and long, cloth stockings called **hose**. In the 1800's, men began to wear suits with long pants and fitted jackets. They wore cloaks or overcoats over them.

▶ In the 1850's, huge stiffened underskirts called crinolines were in fashion. The artist who drew this thought crinolines were a silly fashion.

Unusual Clothing

In Europe, people have worn some very strangely shaped clothing. In the 1600's, people wore huge frilled collars called **ruffs**. Two hundred years later, women's skirts were held out by stiffened hoops that supported large underskirts called **crinolines**. These were like large lampshades and they made it very difficult for women to sit down!

Pants and Skirts

In Central Asia and the USSR, pants have been worn for a long time by both men and women. In the Greek and Roman Empires, only farmers and slaves wore pants. In hot countries, men first wore skirts draped around their waists. Today, many women all over the world wear pants, but not many men still wear skirts.

Skirts

In ancient Egypt, men and women wore only one garment. This was a skirt. Later, women wore tunics. The tunics became longer and looked more like dresses. Men's skirts grew longer too. They were divided in the middle. They became loose cotton pants. In Fiji, Malaysia, and Scotland, men still wear skirts. The Scottish national dress for men is a kilt.

In many Asian countries, like India and Sri Lanka, men still wear cloth wrapped around their waists. The Indian **dhoti** is a length of cloth made of light cotton. It can be worn loosely like a skirt. During work, the back part is usually pulled through the legs and tucked into the waist. This makes loose pants.

Pants

Roman soldiers first saw pants when they went to war in Northern Europe. The people who lived in what is now Germany, France, and Britain wore them. The Romans did not copy the style. They thought that only wild, uncivilized people wore pants.

▼ This papyrus from ancient Egypt shows that the men wore just a short skirt. This was made by wrapping a cloth around the waist. Some of the men have fastened this with a belt.

dhoti

short
breeches
late
1500's

French
1600's

late 1800's

In Europe, over 500 years ago, men who worked on the land wore loose, baggy pants. The landowners wore tightly fitted pants. This showed that the landowner did not have to work on the land. About a hundred years later, knee-length pants were worn.

Pants for Women

In Asian countries, women have always worn pants. In Europe, women did not wear them until over a hundred years ago. The idea of women wearing pants was shocking. In 1851, an American woman, named Amelia Bloomer, shocked people by wearing baggy pants under a short skirt. These "bloomers" caused an uproar.

Very few women dared to wear pants in western countries, in public, until the 1940's. Then, during World War II, women had to work in factories and on the land. Pants were much easier to work in than a skirt. Since that time, more and more women have worn pants.

▲ These drawings show how pants have changed. At first men wore a cloth around their waists. Then to make moving around easier, they tied a piece of cloth between their legs.

▲ Amelia Bloomer owned a newspaper in New York in the 1800's. At that time, women's clothes were hard to move around in. She used her newspaper to encourage women to wear "bloomers."

Underwear and Night Clothes

Underwear was first worn to keep the outer clothing clean. It also stopped the garment from scratching the skin. Until about 500 years ago, few people had special clothing to sleep in. Most people slept in their underwear, or without any clothing at all.

Women's Underwear

Some garments need underwear to keep them in place. Indian women wear ankle-length underskirts. Their short-sleeved tops are called **cholis**. The sari is wrapped around the underskirt and tucked into it. The long end of the sari is draped over one shoulder of the choli.

Roman women wore sleeveless tunics under their clothing. For many years, these tunics, called **shifts**, were the only underwear women wore throughout Europe. Then, they began to wear underskirts, called **petticoats**, for extra warmth. Roman women also wore a kind of bra. This idea was not copied. The type we know today was first worn only about seventy years ago.

About 300 years ago, French women wore long silk pants. These pants were called **drawers** and they were worn under skirts. The style was copied from the one worn in Asia. People thought it was wrong for women to wear pants even though they were hidden. Most women in Europe did not wear short underpants until about eighty years ago.

Men's Underwear

Men who lived in cold countries were the first to wear undergarments. Over 800 years ago, men in Europe wore undershirts and short, baggy drawers. In the 1800's, men often wore woollen undershirts. They also had ankle-length underpants called "long johns." Today, most men wear short underpants and sleeveless or short-sleeve undershirts.

Changing Shapes

Underwear can be used to change the shape of the body. Over 300 years ago, women wore hidden rolls of cloth stuffed with wool. These **farthingales** made their skirts stick out at the hips. In Europe, about 150 years ago, men with skinny legs wore padding to make it appear they had large leg muscles. Later, women's skirts were held out by crinoline hoops, or padded at the back with **bustles**.

▼ Fashions in underwear have changed over the years for men and women.

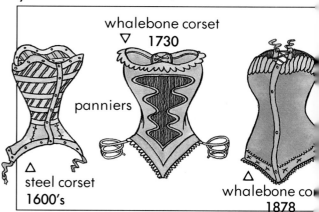

whalebone corset
▽ 1730

panniers

△
steel corset
1600's

△
whalebone co
1878

Night Clothes

About 400 years ago, most people in Europe wore night clothes. Men wore plain shirts and women wore shifts. Both men and women wore nightcaps in bed to keep their heads warm. Three hundred years later, men began to wear shirts and pants to bed. This fashion was copied from garments worn during the day in India. The new outfits were called pajamas.

▲ This cartoon was drawn in 1820. At the time, women used corsets or stays to make their waists very small. It was a very uncomfortable fashion. There was never a machine like this. The artist is just showing how foolish this fashion was.

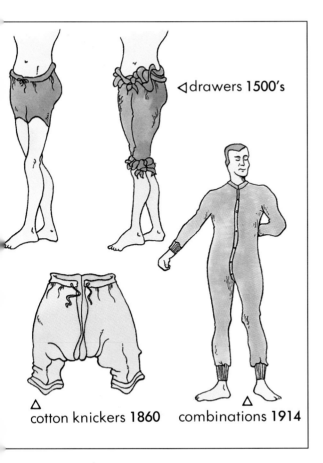

◁drawers 1500's

△
cotton knickers 1860

△
combinations 1914

▼ This is the style of nightdress worn at the beginning of this century. It was made of soft warm fabric, and it was very loose. It was much more comfortable than daytime clothes.

Jewelry and Cosmetics

We know that long ago, people wore jewels and gold for decoration. Gold and precious stones do not decay. Necklaces and rings look just like they did when they were first worn. Many of these things have been found in tombs, or buried under the ground. Often, jewels were worn as charms. Roman boys wore gold necklaces called **bullas** for luck. In Sicily today, some children still wear a kind of bulla. It holds a red coral bead.

In many countries, men and women wore gold and jewels to show that they were rich. Kings and queens wore crowns made from gold and precious stones. Gifts of jewelry were often given to the bride at weddings.

Today, jewelry is seldom made with real stones. It is made of synthetic materials which look like jewels. It is called costume jewelry.

▲ Gold has been used for jewelry for thousands of years. This headdress was made about 5,000 years ago for a queen. It comes from the Middle East. It is made of gold and a stone called lapis lazuli.

▲ This woman is from Pakistan where it is the custom to wear a lot of beautiful jewelry. She is even wearing jewelry in her hair and a jeweled nose pin.

Makeup

For hundreds of years, people have painted their faces. Sometimes, they did this to scare off their enemies. The ancient Britains painted their bodies with blue dye. They made the dye from a plant called **woad**. Native Americans painted their faces before they went into battle. Many other groups did this, too.

In ancient Egypt and Asia, people painted their faces, too. They thought it made them look beautiful. They drew dark lines around their eyes with a black paint called **kohl**. Egyptian women used orange color on their lips and cheeks. They painted their fingers and toenails with a colored varnish. In Egypt, Japan, and later in Europe, women rubbed their faces with white lead. This was very dangerous. Lead is a poison and it eats into the skin.

Face paints and oil for the skin are called cosmetics. The Roman poet, Ovid, wrote a book about healthy cosmetics. He told people to mix eggs, bean flour, and flower roots with honey. The mixture made a paste. The paste was spread on the face to make the skin softer.

About 300 years ago, men and women in Europe wore a great deal of makeup. Often, men wore more makeup than women. The noblemen in France painted their eyes and cheeks, and wore face powder. They grew their fingernails long. This was to show they did not have to work with their hands. Chinese rulers also grew very long nails.

▲ In the past both men and women wore makeup. Often they reddened their lips and cheeks. Sometimes they made their faces white and plucked their eyebrows to make their faces more like a mask.

About one hundred years ago, makeup had gone out of fashion in Europe. Women in Europe and America did not dare to paint their faces or nails. The most girls could do was to bite their lips to make them red! Few women used much makeup until the 1940's. Today, women use as much, or as little, makeup as they wish. Men are beginning to wear it again, too. In Europe and North America, many young men make up their faces. The young pop stars of the music world have led this fashion.

Hats, Hairstyles, and Wigs

People used to think the head was very important. Rulers wore crowns or headdresses on their heads. They wore them to show that they were important people.

People also had to protect their heads from the cold or from the hot sun. They wore hats to do this. In battles, they wore **helmets** to keep their heads safe from injury.

Hats

The first hats were often made from animals hides or feathers. In Africa and North America, bird feathers were worn. The Native Americans thought feathers carried prayers to heaven. Between one hundred and 200 years ago, it was a fashion in Europe to wear ostrich feathers on hats. Women wore these feathers in their hair in the evening.

In cold countries like Tibet or the USSR, hats often have ear flaps. In hot, wet countries like China and Malaysia, straw hats with wide brims keep the sun and the rain off the head. Sometimes, hats were worn for other reasons. In Ancient Greece and Rome, skull caps meant that you were not a slave. You were a free person.

Veils

Many women covered their heads with a veil. In the Middle East and Asia, the veil often covered the face as well. In Europe, women often covered their hair and their chins, but they did not veil their faces. In the 1400's, women wore tall pointed hats called **hennins**. Veils were sewn on to the points. For about another 200 years, both men and women wore hats indoors. Then, in Europe, it became common for men to remove their hats indoors.

⊲ India ⊲ Bolivia ⊲ Canada △ North Thailand ⊲ Europe

We can learn a lot from hats. Some hats tell us that the wearer is an important person. Other hats are traditional, like the bowler hats worn by Bolivian women. In cold countries, people need warm hats of wool or fur. In hot countries, hats help to keep people cool.

Hairstyles and False Hair

Hairstyles have also been changed by fashion. About 3,500 years ago, in the Near East, Assyrian men sometimes wore false beards. In Greece and Rome, men wore their hair short. There were barbershops in Roman towns. Women often curled and frizzed their hair. The Romans also used **bleach** to dye their hair blonde.

In the 1600's, and later, men in Europe used to shave their heads. They wore false hair called wigs. Long curled wigs were made from animal hair. Later, the wigs were tied back in plaits, or pigtails, with bows. Women also wore wigs. Sometimes, they built their own hair up on metal frames to look like a wig. These headdresses often held feathers, model ships, or baskets of fruit! Both men and women put white powder on their hair. In Britain, the government made money out of this style. Every time any hair powder was sold, some money had to be paid to the government as a tax. So powder cost more and more money. Hairstyles soon became plainer!

▲ The fashion in the 1400's was to wear a tall tight-fitting cap or hennin. This woman has covered her hennin with a stiffened veil. No hair was supposed to show, so she shaved her hairline back.

◁ Holland

France 1600's ▷

▲ During the 1780's, the fashion was to have a lot of hair. This was curled, powdered, and decorated with bows and lace. Women also wore hats and bonnets with a lot of trimming.

Head to Toe

Shoes, gloves, and umbrellas are all parts of clothing. They protect our feet, our hands and our heads, from the heat, the cold, and the rain.

Sandals and Shoes

Sandals were the first footwear. They were made by cutting a piece of leaf, hide or wood to the same size as the foot. This made the sole of the sandal. It was tied to the foot, or held on by a toe string.

Simple shoes were made by wrapping leather around the foot. The leather was held with a crisscross thong. Roman women wore woollen foot coverings under their shoes. They were called *soccus*. The word has now become "sock." Native Americans wore soft leather shoes called moccasins. In some countries, shoes were carved from a piece of wood. These wooden shoes, called **clogs**, were strong and heavy. People also wore wooden overshoes to keep their feet dry. The shoes were called **pattens**. They were wooden soles which were strapped over other shoes. When people wore them, they could walk through mud and water. Their feet stayed dry.

▶ The Romans and Greeks wore sandals. These protected the soles of their feet. They kept the feet cool. In cold countries, people needed to keep their feet warm and dry. They wore shoes. Some shoes were made just to look good. They were made of silk or soft kid leather.

Fashions in shoes changed, too. Sometimes, toes were pointed or square. In the 1400's, men wore shoes with long pointed toes. The points were so long that they had to be fastened to the knees so the wearer would not trip! It was not until about 1800 that left and right shoes were made. Before that they could be worn on either foot.

Greek sandals

pointed boots 1400's

man's shoe 1600's

Moroccan slipper

lady's boot late 1800's

Japanese shoes

◀ We wear gloves for many reasons. Some gloves keep our hands warm. Other gloves keep them clean or dry. These gloves are not meant to do any of those things. They are fashionable gloves worn for decoration. Some of the gloves have no fingers. They were worn indoors.

Umbrellas

The word umbrella means a "shade maker." The first umbrellas were used in China over 3,000 years ago. They were held to shade the Chinese rulers from the sun. For a long time, umbrellas, or **parasols**, were used only as sunshades. Then, in 1750, a British man began a new fashion. He held an umbrella up to keep the rain off his head!

Gloves

People tied cloth or fur around their hands to keep them warm. This was the first kind of glove. These **mittens** covered all the fingers together. They were difficult to work in. In Asia, gloves were unknown. There, sleeves were made with long cuffs to fold down in cold weather. In other countries, sewn or knitted gloves with fingers were used. Sometimes, the ends of the fingers were left uncovered to make work easier. Gloves were often embroidered, or trimmed with lace and jewels.

Longer gloves covered the wrists and arms as well as the hands. These were called **gauntlets**. Leather gauntlets were worn by people who used hunting birds. The birds perched on their wrists. Metal gauntlets were a part of suits of **armor**. They were worn in battle.

▼ This government official is from Chad in West Africa. The decorated umbrella is carried beside him to show that he is an important man.

Buttons and Bows

Fur and hide clothes were first held together by thorns, or by long, sharp bones. Then, when people began to use metal, they made pins. The pin was pushed in and out of the cloth. Then, a **clasp** at the back of the pin held it safely shut. Pins were decorated. They were bent into shapes, or made to hold colored stones. These pins are called brooches.

The Greeks and Romans used pins and brooches to fasten their draped clothes. The Celtic peoples of Northern Europe pinned their cloaks at the shoulder with fine brooches. They were round and were often made from gold. Sometimes, they were decorated with jewels and **enamel**.

Buttons

In the northern parts of Britain, skeletons have been found wearing rows of buttons down their fronts. The buttons are carved from animal bone. They may be all that remains of clothing that was worn 5,000 years ago. Buttons do not appear to have been used in many places until about 700 years ago.

▲ People have used buckles for fastening belts and waistbands for centuries. This buckle is over 1,000 years old. It was made by Anglo-Saxon people in Britain. It is solid gold and weighs nearly a pound. It is decorated very skillfully with a snake design.

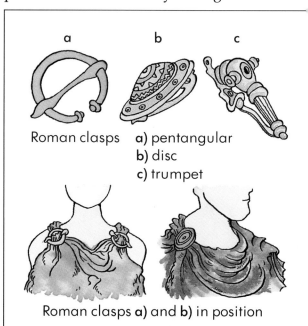

Roman clasps   a) pentangular
               b) disc
               c) trumpet

Roman clasps a) and b) in position

Between 600 and 700 years ago, clothing fitted more tightly. Buttons began to be used to fasten gowns and sleeves. They were also sewn on to garments for decoration. By the 1700's, buttons were often made from silver and precious stones. Later, long rows of buttons were used not only on clothes, but on boots and gloves as well. Special **button hooks** were sold to help fasten them.

Ribbons and Bows

Clothing can also be fastened by tying the ends of a piece of cloth together. This makes a knot. Native American clothing was often tied together with thongs made from thin strips of animal hide. In hot countries, simple garments were tied together with plaited grass.

▼ Buttons and bows have been used to fasten clothes for thousands of years.

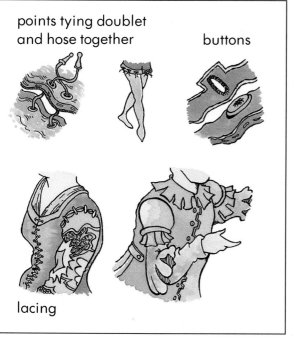

points tying doublet and hose together

buttons

lacing

Over 400 years ago, clothing in Europe was often tied with lengths of ribbon, called **points**. Sometimes, the points were tied in a bow. They decorated a sleeve or a pant leg. Since then, bows have often been used to decorate clothing. Shoelaces and apron strings are still tied together with bows.

Zippers

About 300 to 400 years ago, clothing began to be fastened with metal hooks and eyes. Hooking them took a long time. In the 1890's, an American, named Whitcomb Judson, invented a way to lock metal hooks and eyes together quickly. He used these early zippers to fasten rubber boots for women and galoshes for men. The Hook and Eye Co of New Jersey sold them as "C-Curity." They did not sell well because they did not always stay together!

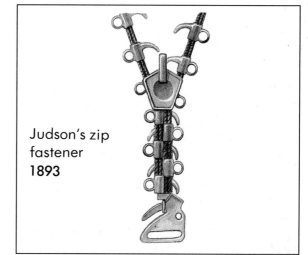

Judson's zip fastener 1893

▲ Hooks and eyes have been used to fasten clothes sinces the 1500's. At the end of the 1800's, the first zipper was invented. Today, we often use zippers, and they are now most often made of plastic.

Protective Clothing

Some jobs need special kinds of clothing. They may be worn to keep people safe or clean.

Protection in Battle

Soldiers need special clothing to protect them. Greek soldiers' tunics were made of leather and metal. Their helmets were trimmed with colored horsehair. Over 700 years ago, special tunics were worn. These were made by linking small rings of metal together. This was called **chain mail**. Two hundred years later, armor was made from flat plates of metal. These were tied together.

Today, soldiers need light clothing that is bulletproof. They also wear clothes which make them hard to see. This is called **camouflage**. The clothes are green and brown and black.

Waterproof Clothing

Most people do not like to wear wet clothes. People learned how to keep water out of their garments. They rubbed them with linseed oil. Oilskins were used for hundreds of years. Sailors found oilskin very useful at sea. British sailors are sometimes called "Jack Tars." This is because their clothes used to be made from **canvas**. The canvas was covered with tar.

◀ These suits of armor are from Japan. They date from the 1700's. They are made of iron and wood, and then painted with lacquer.

◀ Modern fire fighting garments work very well. These people can stand very close to a gas explosion. These garments are heatproof.

Keeping Clean

Until about 200 years ago, many people did not know that dirt spread diseases. Patients died because hospitals were dirty. Today, when operations are going on, everyone wears very clean clothing. The nurses and doctors wear long gowns and they cover their mouths with masks. They wear thin rubber gloves and often use paper caps and masks. The gloves, caps and masks are used once and then thrown away, to get rid of any germs.

About 200 years ago, Charles Macintosh, a Scottish chemist, made cloth coats which were lined with rubber. People in Britain called them Macs or Macintoshes after him. Because they kept the rain out, we say they are waterproof. In the United States, we call them raincoats.

People who make and sell food also need to keep clean. They must cover their hair while they work. In many factories, the workers wear special hats, gloves, and overalls. These garments, protect the workers. People who work in places where medicine is made must be extra careful.

Heatproof Clothing

People who work in hot places with furnaces have to keep cool. People who fight fires need to be protected. In 1879, **asbestos** cloth was first made. This could protect people against heat. Today, special suits are made. They have a metal in the fabric. It is called **aluminum**. These suits do not burn. They are fireproof. Some suits have special pipes in them. The pipes are used for breathing. Firemen can wear these suits right inside a fire. They will still be safe.

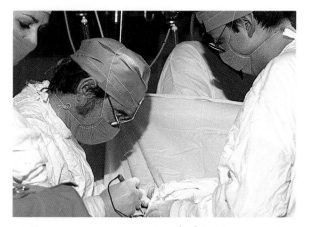

▲ Doctors wear protective clothing in operating rooms. Before the doctors wear them, the garments are treated to kill all the germs.

Special Clothing

Clothing can tell us a lot about a person. It can tell us what job a person does. Sometimes, clothing tells us how important a person is.

Rulers and priests often wear special clothing and colors. Maori chiefs in New Zealand wore cloaks made of feathers. These were not needed to keep them warm. They were worn as a sign of power. In Africa, chiefs wore leopard skins. Native American chiefs wore eagle feathers. The eagle is one of the largest and fiercest of birds. The braver the chief, the more eagle feathers he wore. Important Romans were allowed to wear togas with purple edges. Only the Emperor could wear a toga that was dyed purple all over.

Today, kings and queens wear crowns and robes on special days. Leaders of towns or cities in Europe wear cloaks and special necklaces or brooches. On special days, Christian bishops wear tall hats called **mitres**. Sometimes, religious garments are very simple. Buddhist monks shave their heads and wear orange robes. Christian monks and nuns dress in dark-colored garments. These people dress alike to show that they belong to a group.

▶ These are Buddhist monks from Tibet. The monks are wearing robes for a ceremony. There are several groups of Buddhist monks in Tibet. These belong to a group called the Yellow Hat sect.

Uniforms

Sometimes, groups of people dress alike. They wear a special garment. They are wearing uniforms. Uniform means "the same." Soldiers first wore uniforms to show which side they were on. Athletes often wear uniforms for the same reason. The athletes and the people watching them can tell each side easily. Police officers wear uniforms, too. Nurses in hospitals wear uniforms. They both wear uniforms so they can be seen easily if they are needed.

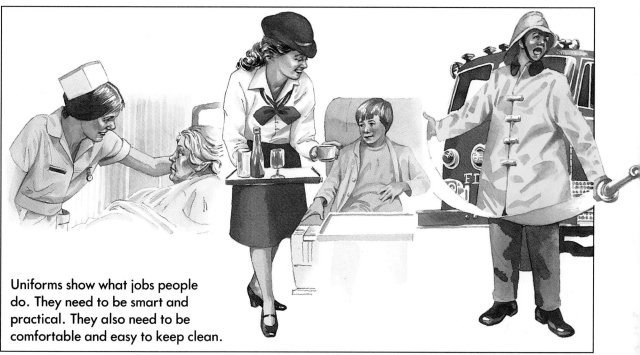

Uniforms show what jobs people do. They need to be smart and practical. They also need to be comfortable and easy to keep clean.

Weddings and Funerals

People wear special clothes for weddings and funerals. In many European countries and in North America, brides often wear long white dresses at weddings. In Japan, too, women may wear white kimonos when they get married. In some parts of India, brides wear red saris.

In China, white is worn as a sign of sadness. White garments are worn at funerals. In many other countries, people wear black when someone dies.

▶ Weddings are always a time for wearing special clothes. This is a Hindu wedding in Madras. Often, a Hindu bride wears a red sari. This bride has on a golden sari. She carries a special flame. The wedding is performed in front of this flame.

Casual Wear

When people are not at work, they like to relax. Some people play sports. Other people go on long walks or sail boats. Many people like to work in their gardens, or sit and rest. They wear clothing that is comfortable and easy to wash.

Special clothing for sports has been worn for a long time. In Sicily, there is a picture that is 2,000 years old. It shows Roman girls in a gym. They are wearing bikinis and one of them is holding weights. They can move around easily.

Garments for sport have not always been easy to move around in. In the 1880's, women played tennis in long skirts and hats! At the beginning of the 1900's, women wanted to ride bicycles. Their long skirts got caught in the wheels. To avoid this, they began to wear divided skirts, or baggy knee-length pants called **knickerbockers**.

▼ Bikinis are nothing new. This picture comes from a Roman villa. We can see that Roman women wore bikinis to do gymnastics.

▶ Today, both women and men wear comfortable sportswear. It was not always like that. This is a tennis game in 1880. Women had to play in long skirts and tight jackets. Over the years, women began wearing shorter and looser clothing.

Garments for sport are also worn to protect the body. Football players wear huge, padded uniforms and helmets. Jockeys who ride racehorses wear hard hats. They also wear bright silk shirts. These help people to see who is winning the race.

▲ This advertisement for bicycles was printed in 1895. The young woman is wearing knickerbockers. It was the latest fashion for biking. It was a very daring fashion to wear when most women kept their legs covered right down to their ankles.

Clothing and the Seaside

Over one hundred years ago, swimming in the sea became a fashion. Doctors said it was very healthy. People were very shy about swimming. So, they were carried to the edge of the water in tall wagons. Then, they stepped into the water behind a screen. They wore their underwear in the water.

Later, more practical swimwear was designed. Women's bathing suits had knee-length skirts. Men's bathing suits had long legs and sleeves. In the 1930's, sunbathing became a new craze. Bathing suits no longer covered the arms and legs, but they were still one piece. The two-piece bathing suit, or bikini, came into fashion in the 1950's.

Evening Dress

Sometimes, when people go out in the evening they like to wear special clothing. Women often wear long dresses and jewels. They want to look elegant. Men often wear dinner jackets and bow ties. They may even wear jackets with long "tails." This style of dressing is called "evening dress" and is worn to special evening events.

Making and Selling Clothing

Long ago, only rich people could buy silks and furs from other lands. Weavers sold rough, homespun cloth at markets and fairs. Sometimes, people took the cloth home to sew. Sometimes, they paid a tailor or a dressmaker to sew for them. Hats, gloves and shoes are difficult to make. They were sold in stores or at open air markets by the people who made them.

Pins, ribbons, and buckles were sold by travelers called **pedlars**. Pedlars did not make these goods. They bought them cheaply from other traders. They displayed them on their pushcarts at markets, or went door-to-door.

By the early 1800's, many people in Europe had moved from the country to work in towns. The poorest people who lived in towns hardly ever bought new clothing. Instead, their clothing was second-hand and came from markets. Other people in towns did not have time to make their own clothing. They bought their clothing from a tailor or a dressmaker.

In the stores, customers were shown dressed dolls, or colored pictures of the latest fashions. When they had chosen the style they liked, the dressmaker made it in their size. Until the mid-1850's, dressmakers had to make their own paper patterns and to do all the sewing by hand.

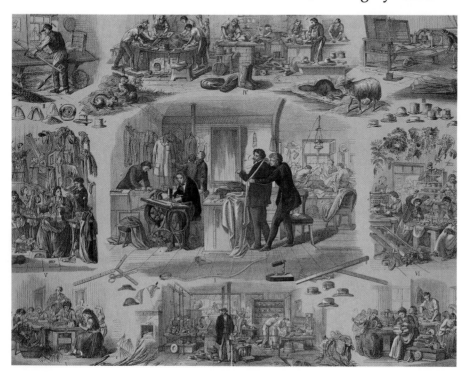

◀ In the past, all clothing was made by hand. In the 1800's things began to change. This picture shows hatters, milliners, and tailors in 1871. Most are working by hand. Some are already using machines.

Clothing Factories

In 1830, a French tailor, Barthélemy Thimmonier, set up a factory in Paris. He had eighty sewing machines. He wanted to make clothing for the French army. People thought the factory would take work away from handworkers. His machines were smashed. In the United States, sewing machines changed the old methods of working. They meant that clothes could be made in factories. Instead of buying a fabric and a pattern, people could buy ready-made clothing.

People were paid very low wages for making clothing. The factories were often dark and unhealthy places. There was not much room for the workers. Sometimes, people were given machines to use at home. They were paid "by the piece" for each garment. They had to work long hours to make enough money to live on.

These factories, or **sweatshops**, were often the only places where people could find work. In 1890, a newspaper reporter visited the East Side of New York. He said the streets were filled with "the whirr of a thousand sewing machines, working from dawn until mind and muscle gave out together." In 1911, a shirt factory called the Triangle Waist Co. caught fire. Most of the workers died. After this, people started to make the factories safer.

▼ In the past, dressmakers cut clothes out one by one. This machine can cut many garments at once. It makes the job faster and cheaper.

▲ This is a modern dressmaking factory. The workers use sewing machines. They are modern machines. Unlike the old sweatshops, the factory is light and clean. However, jobs people have to do are still much the same.

Children's clothing

Clothing for young children was first made over 200 years ago. Before that time, children were usually dressed in baby clothes until they were three or four years old. Then, they were dressed in the same styles as their parents.

Baby Clothes

In many countries, babies were often wrapped tightly in cloth. Strips of cloth bound their arms and legs to their sides. People thought that babies needed these clothes to make their bones grow straight. Babies wore this cloth for about nine months. In some parts of Eastern Europe, and among some Native American tribes, these **swaddling clothes** are still used.

Then, over one hundred years ago, babies began to be dressed in long dresses and shawls in North America and Europe. Boys stayed in dresses until they were about four years old.

Special Children's Clothing

In the 1800's, boys often wore sailor suits or knee-length pants. They also wore a cap. A boy's first pair of long pants made him feel very grown-up. Young girls wore **smocks** over their dresses. They also wore dresses with long **pantalettes** underneath. Older girls wore ankle-length skirts. They could wear their hair pinned up. It was a sign that they were old enough to marry.

▲ This little girl is wearing traditional Japanese clothing. Children in Japan do not usually dress like this, although they used to.

▶ These children's portrait was painted in 1840. The youngest is a boy, but he is wearing a dress. The little girl is still wearing a very short skirt. Her older sister and brother are already in grownup clothes.

Some children were dressed in embroidered silks. Their garments were decorated with lacy collars and jewels. It cannot have been easy to play in such clothing.

Most children wore simple clothing, made by a relative or a friend. They wore clothing that they could play and work in.

Fashions for Young People

Fashions for young people are a new idea. In the 1950's, teenagers had more money to spend than ever before. They began to develop fashions of their own. In the late 1950's, in Britain, many young men wore long jackets, tight pants and greased their hair back. They were called "Teddy Boys" because they wore the fashions of the days of King Edward VII.

Young people's fashions are often meant to shock their elders. Young men's long hair shocked people in the

1960's. Girls' miniskirts, which were very short, shocked people in the 1960's and 1970's. Spikey, brightly colored hair, or no hair at all, shocked people in the 1970's and 1980's. Often, these "shocking" fashions are like fashions which have been worn in the past and shocked no one then.

▼ New fashions spring up all the time. Some are more popular than others. Some of the most unusual clothing is for young people.

Quiz

How much can you remember? Try to do this quiz and use the index and glossary to help you check your answers.

1. Here are the scrambled names of four famous fashion designers. Unscramble the letters to find out who they are. **Clue:**They all worked in Paris.

   a) TOWRH, b) RIDO,   c) NERITB, d) HAECNL

2. Match the descriptions (a) to (f) with the words numbered (1) to (6) below them.
   a) A skirt held out by hoops
   b) A dark eye paint
   c) A South American cape, put on over the head
   d) A woman's underskirt
   e) A bishop's hat
   f) A head covering worn by men in India

   1) poncho
   2) turban
   3) crinoline
   4) kohl
   5) petticoat
   6) mitre

3. Complete the following sentences with (a), (b), (c), or (d):
   1) A method of softening animal hides by soaking them in a liquid is called
   a) tattooing.   c) tailoring.
   b) tanning.   d) draping.

2) One of the first tools for making thread was called a
   a) spindle.   c) point.
   b) hennin.   d) distaff.

3) In the Middle East, some women cover their faces with
   a) parasols.   c) veils.
   b) wigs.   d) togas.

4) Gauntlets cover
   a) the legs and feet.
   b) the nose and ears.
   c) the wrist and arm.
   d) the heel and toes.

5) Farthingales were rolls of padding worn under
   a) jackets.   c) shoes.
   b) skirts.   d) hats.

4. Which word does not belong in each group? Why?
   a) breeches, bloomers, doublet, drawers
   b) sari, toga, jacket, sarong
   c) wig, sandal, crown, helmet
   d) silk, wool, nylon, cotton
   e) petticoat, cloak, corset, shift

5. Are these statements true or false?
   a) Rayon is a natural material.
   b) Felt comes from the bark of a tree.
   c) Weaving is done on a loom.
   d) Buttons were not used until the 1800's.
   e) Pattens were wooden overshoes on an iron ring.

6. Who
   a) shocked people in 1851 by wearing trousers?
   b) gave his name to what the British call raincoats?

c) sold the first sewing machines for use in the home?

d) invented the first zipper?

7. What

a) machine did James Hargreaves invent?

b) thread was invented in the United States in 1937?

c) color is used as a sign of sadness in China?

d) is the name for a charm which protects a person against evil?

8. Why

a) were British sailors called Jack Tars?

b) did Roman boys wear bullas?

c) were babies dressed in swaddling clothes?

d) do some Arab women wear veils?

9. Each of these sentences includes a piece of clothing. The name of the piece of clothing is scrambled. Unscramble the letters to find the correct word:

a) Soldiers wore METHESL on their heads to protect them.

b) MONOIKS are loose robes worn in Japan.

c) The IKIBIN is a two-piece bathing suit.

d) Native Americans wore CSNISOCAM on their feet, made from soft leather.

e) Women in India wear a short-sleeved blouse called a HLCOI under their saris.

10. Which part of the body is covered by:
a) a clog? b) a mitten? c) hose?
d) a shawl? e) a hennin?

Answers

1. (a) Worth,(b) Dior, (c) Bertin, (d) Chanel

2. (a) 3, (b) 6, (c) 1, (d) 5, (e) 4, (f) 2

3. (1) b, (2) d, (3) c, (4) c, (5) b

4. (a) doublet (all the others are types of pants)
(b) jacket (all the others are draped clothes)
(c) sandal (all the others are worn on the head)
(d) nylon (all the others are natural materials)
(e) cloak (all the others are types of underwear)

5. (a) false, (b) false, (c) true, (d) false, (e) true

6. (a) Amelia Bloomer, (b) Charles Macintosh,

7. (a) the Spinning Jenny, (b) nylon, (c) white, (d) amulet

8. (a) because their clothes were painted with tar to make them waterproof (b) to keep away evil spirits and the bring them good luck (c) because people believed that it would make their arms and legs grow straight (d) so that no man, except their husbands, can see their faces

9. (a) helmets, (b) kimonos, (c) bikini, (d) moccasins, (e) choli

10. (a) the foot, (b) the hand, (c) the legs, (d) the shoulders, (e) the head

Glossary

aluminum: a metal which is very light. It can be made very thin and used in fireproof material.
amulet: something worn as a charm to protect against evil.
armor: clothing or a covering of wood or metal worn as a protection against weapons.
asbestos: a mineral found in the ground. It is made up of fibers. Asbestos can be woven to make a cloth that does not burn.

bleach: a liquid that takes the color out of other substances.
breeches: pants cut off just below the knee.
bulla: a round metal ornament worn on a chain by Roman children. Bullas were also used to seal documents.
bustle: the padding worn inside a woman's skirt at the bottom of her back. A bustle gave extra fullness and shape to the skirt.
button hook: a small hand held tool with a hook on the end. The hook was used to pull buttons through buttonholes.

camouflage: the color, pattern, or shape which helps to hide an object in its surroundings.
canvas: a strong, heavy cloth usually made of cotton. It is used for making tents and sails.
cellulose: a substance that plants are made of.
chain mail: a type of armor. It is made from connected links of metal. It protects the wearer in battle and allows freedom of movement.
chemical: any substance which can change when joined or mixed with another substance.
choli: a round necked, waist-length blouse with short sleeves. It is worn under a sari by women in India.
clasp: the fastening on a necklace or a brooch. On a brooch the clasp is the pin which attaches the brooch to clothing.
clog: a shoe carved out of a piece of wood or with a wooden bottom or sole.
cocoon: the silken case which protects the pupa of a moth and other insects.
crinoline: an underskirt with different-sized hoops attached to it. The skirt that is worn over it stands away from the legs in a bell shape.

Crusades: a series of wars between European Christians and the Turks in the Holy Land, between the years 1000 and 1400.
dhoti: a piece of cotton material worn like a skirt by Hindu men in India.
distaff: the wooden stick that holds wool for spinning. The fibers of wool are then pulled from it to be spun into threads.
doublet: a tightly-fitting piece of clothing for the top of the body. It was short and worn with or without sleeves.
drape: a way of hanging cloth in loose folds over an object.
drawers: loose underpants. Drawers are like baggy pants.

embroidery: decorative needlework. The designs are usually stitched on cloth.
enamel: a glossy substance that has been put on metal by heating and melting.

fabric: a cloth made by weaving or knitting.
farthingale: a padded hoop sometimes made of whalebone. This was worn around the waist, and made skirts stick out at the sides.
felt: a kind of thick cloth made by pressing hair or wool flat.
fiber: a hair-like or thread-like part of something. Cloth is made of fibers.

gauntlet: a glove with a large cuff which protects the hand, wrist and lower arm. A gauntlet was often covered with armor.

helmet: a strengthened covering designed to protect the head.
hennin: a tall, usually pointed, woman's hat with a piece of thin material hanging from its top, worn during the Middle Ages.
homespun: a simple cloth or material made in the home and not in a factory.
hose: tight-fitting coverings or stockings for the legs or feet. Hose was usually made of fine material like silk or wool.

industry: the work of making or producing goods, often in a factory.

kilt: a short, pleated skirt. The kilt worn by men in Scotland is usually checked, or woven in a plaid pattern, known as tartan.

kimono: a long, loose robe with wide sleeves worn in Japan. It is usually held in place by a wide sash, called an obi.

knickerbockers: loose, short trousers which are gathered in at the knee. They were sometimes called "knickers."

kohl: a fine black powder used for darkening the eyelids. It is widely used in India, Pakistan, and the Middle East.

loom: a machine for weaving thread into cloth.

mitre: a tall headdress, worn by bishops, which is split into two peaks at the top. A mitre is worn by bishops.

mitten: a kind of glove which covers the whole hand. It does not have separate covers for each finger.

moccasin: a shoe made out of pieces of deerskin or other soft leather stitched together. Moccasins were originally worn by Native Americans

natural materials: materials made from animals or things which live and grow in the world around us.

nitric acid: a strong, burning liquid made by mixing different chemicals. It is poisonous and dangerous.

pantalettes: long, loose underpants with a frill at the bottom of each leg. They come below the bottom of the dress.

parasol: an umbrella used to give shade from the sun. Parasols are usually small and light.

patten: a thick wooden sole often mounted on an iron ring. A patten was attached to a shoe to raise it out of the mud.

pedlar: a person who goes from place to place carrying things for sale.

petticoat: underskirt which fastens around the waist. It is worn under skirts and dresses.

point: a thin piece of cloth, lace, or cord. It is used for fastening clothes or for tying two pieces of material together.

poncho: a blanket or piece of material with a hole made for the head. The poncho hangs over the shoulders like a cloak.

ruff: a frill worn around the neck. Ruffs are usually made of stiffened material gathered into many even folds.

sari: a long piece of cotton or other light material often worn as the main garment by Hindu women. It is folded around the body with one end over the head or shoulder.

sarong: a long cloth wrapped around the waist like a skirt or tucked under the armpits. A sarong is worn in Malaysia by men and women.

shift: a loose, shapeless dress.

shuttle: a small boat-shaped tool used in weaving.

smock: a loose, shirt-like garment which covers other clothing. Today smocks are usually worn by children.

spindle: a rod which has two thin ends. A spindle is used to twist fibers to make thread.

swaddling clothes: strips of cloth which are tied tightly around a baby to keep it from moving.

sweatshop: a factory or shop where people have to work in poor conditions for very long hours and for very low wages.

synthetic: describes a material produced by combining chemicals.

tailoring: making clothes to fit exactly.

tanning: a way of changing animal hides into soft leather by soaking them in a liquid. The liquid is made from oak bark or other vegetable mixtures.

tattoo: a picture or pattern permanently marked on the skin. Tattooing is done by pricking the skin with needles dipped in colored inks.

toga: a piece of woollen material worn by the Romans. A toga hung loosely and covered the whole body except for the head and right arm.

tunic: a garment which hangs straight down from the shoulders to the upper half of the legs. It usually has no sleeves.

turban: a covering for the head made by winding a long length of cloth around a cap or the head.

warp: the threads stretched from the top to the bottom of a loom in weaving.

weft: the threads which run across and through the warp threads in weaving.

woad: a substance from a plant of the same name. Woad colors and stains things blue.

yarn a thread made by twisting fibres.

Index